Pebble® Plus

Animal Offspring

Gorillas and Their Infants

Revised Edition

by Margaret Hall

CAPSTONE PRESS
a capstone imprint

Pebble Plus is published by Capstone Press,
1710 Roe Crest Drive,
North Mankato, Minnesota 56003
www.mycapstone.com

Library of Congress Cataloging-in-Publication Data
Names: Hall, Margaret, 1947- author. Title: Gorillas and their
infants : a 4D book / by Margaret Hall.
Description: Revised edition. | North Mankato, Minnesota :
Capstone Press, a Capstone imprint, [2018] | Series: Pebble plus.
Animal offspring | Audience: Ages 4-8.
Identifiers: LCCN 2017037872 (print) | LCCN 2017054106
(ebook) | ISBN 9781543508642 (eBook PDF) | ISBN
9781543508246 (hardcover) | ISBN 9781543508369 (pbk.)
Subjects: LCSH: Gorilla--Infancy--Juvenile literature. | Parental
behavior in animals--Juvenile literature.
Classification: LCC QL737.P96 (ebook) | LCC QL737.P96 H355
2018 (print) | DDC 599.884/139--dc23
LC record available at https://lccn.loc.gov/2017037872

Editorial Credits
Gina Kammer, editor; Sarah Bennett, designer; Morgan Walters,
media researcher; Katy LaVigne, production specialist

Photo Credits
Shutterstock: abxyz, right 20, blojfo, 19, Edwin Butter, left 20,
left 21, Fiona Ayerst, 7, GUDKOV ANDREY, Cover, islavicek, 13,
Kiki Dohmeier, 17, LMspencer, 15, meunierd, right 21, Nick Fox,
11, Simon Eeman, 3, 5, Stayer, 9

Note to Parents and Teachers

The Animal Offspring set supports national science standards
related to life sciences. This book describes and illustrates
gorillas and their infants. The images support early readers in
understanding the text. The repetition of words and phrases
helps early readers learn new words. This book also introduces
early readers to subject-specific vocabulary words, which
are defined in the Glossary section. Early readers may need
assistance to read some words and to use the Table of Contents,
Glossary, Read More, Internet Sites, Critical Thinking Questions,
and Index sections of the book.

Table of Contents

Gorillas

Gorillas are strong mammals. Young gorillas are called infants. Gorillas and their infants live in Africa.

Gorillas live in family groups called troops. A male gorilla is a silverback. A silverback mates with a female gorilla.

The Infant

A female gorilla usually gives birth to one infant.

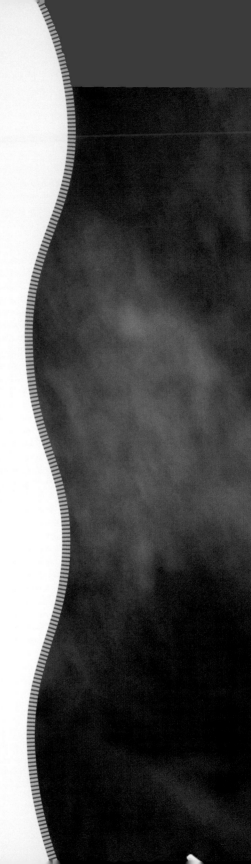

Infants drink milk

from their mothers.

Infants sometimes ride on the backs of their mothers.

Growing Up

Infants grow and become young gorillas. Young gorillas play and climb.

Young gorillas learn
to find food.
Gorillas eat plants
and bark.

Young gorillas leave the troop after about eight years. Then they live with a new troop.

Watch Gorillas Grow

birth

adult after
about ten years

21

Glossary

Africa—one of the seven continents of the world

infant—a very young animal; a gorilla infant depends on its mother for 3 to 5 years

mammal—a warm-blooded animal that has a backbone; mammals have hair or fur and feed milk to their young; gorillas have thick hair

mate—to join together to produce young

silverback—an adult male gorilla; silverbacks have gray or silver hair on their backs

troop—a group of animals that lives or moves together; a troop works together to teach young gorillas how to live and find food

Read More

Jones, Elton. *Gorillas Work Together.* New York: PowerKids Press, 2018.

Macheske, Felicia. *Brainy and Brawny: Gorilla.* Guess What? Ann Arbor, Mich.: Cherry Lake Publishing, 2017.

Ward, Finn. *Gorillas at the Zoo.* New York: Gareth Stevens Publishing, 2016.

Internet Sites

Use FactHound to find Internet sites related to this book.

Visit *www.facthound.com*

Just type 9781543508246 and go.

Check out projects, games and lots more at
www.capstonekids.com

Critical Thinking Questions

1. What kinds of things do young gorillas do?

2. Where in this book can you find out why male gorillas are called silverbacks?

3. How does a mother gorilla care for her infant?

Index